HOME for the HOLIDAYS

Celebrate with **ALDI's**® *festive baking recipes and crafts*

Visit us at
www.ALDI.com

Some of the products listed in this publication may be in limited distribution or only available seasonally.

Pictured on the front cover *(clockwise from top left):* Chocolate Mint Fluff Roll *(page 82)*, Cherry, Almond & Chocolate Breakfast Wreath *(page 54)*, Cocoa Crinkle Sandwiches *(page 22)* and Happy Farms® Buttery Almond Cutouts *(page 8)*.

Craft pictured on the front cover *(center):* Beaded Ornament Covers *(page 77)*.

Pictured on the back cover *(left to right):* Sweet Harvest® Icicle Ornaments *(page 14)* and Festive Fudge Blossoms *(page 6)*.

Ingredient photography by Shaughnessy MacDonald, Inc.

Craft Designers: Jill D. Evans *(pages 30, 31 and 89)*, Trena Hegdahl *(page 60)*, Kathy Lamancusa *(page 76)* and Lucie Sinkler *(page 77)*.

ISBN: 1-4127-2271-3

Manufactured in USA.

8 7 6 5 4 3 2 1

Microwave Cooking: Microwave ovens vary in wattage. Use the cooking times as guidelines and check for doneness before adding more time.

Table of Contents

Crafts

ALDI® is an international retailer specializing in a select assortment of high-quality, private label products at the lowest possible prices. Quality, taste and satisfaction are always DOUBLE* guaranteed at **ALDI**®. We're so confident about the quality of our products we guarantee you'll be satisfied too!

*Excludes non-food Special Purchase items and alcohol.

CHAPTER 1

Santa's Cookies

Festive Fudge Blossoms

Makes 4 dozen cookies

¼ cup (½ stick) Happy Farms® butter, softened
1 box (18.5 ounces) Baker's Corner® Devil's food cake mix
1 Goldhen® egg, lightly beaten
2 tablespoons water
¾ to 1 cup finely chopped Southern Grove® walnuts
48 chocolate star candies or candy kisses

1. Preheat oven to 350°F. Cut butter into cake mix in large bowl with pastry blender or 2 knives until mixture resembles coarse crumbs. Add egg and water; stir until well blended.

2. Shape dough into ¾-inch balls; roll in walnuts, pressing nuts gently into dough. Place about 2 inches apart on ungreased cookie sheets.

3. Bake cookies 8 minutes or until puffed and nearly set. Place chocolate star in center of each cookie; bake 1 minute. Cool 2 minutes on cookie sheets. Remove cookies to wire racks; cool completely.

Happy Farms® Buttery Almond Cutouts

Makes about 3 dozen cookies

1½ cups Sweet Harvest® granulated sugar
1 cup (2 sticks) Happy Farms® butter, softened
¾ cup Friendly Farms sour cream
2 Goldhen® eggs
3 teaspoons almond extract, divided
1 teaspoon Spice Club® pure vanilla
4⅓ cups Grandma's Best® all-purpose flour
1 teaspoon Baker's Corner® baking powder
1 teaspoon Baker's Corner® baking soda
½ teaspoon Sebree® salt
2 cups Sweet Harvest®
    powdered sugar
2 tablespoons Friendly Farms milk
1 tablespoon Baker's Corner®
    light corn syrup
Assorted food colorings

1. Beat granulated sugar and butter in large bowl with electric mixer at medium speed until light and fluffy. Add sour cream, eggs, 2 teaspoons almond extract and vanilla; beat until smooth. Add flour, baking powder, baking soda and salt; beat just until well blended.

2. Shape dough into 4 equal discs. Wrap each disc tightly with Kwik-N-Fresh® plastic wrap. Refrigerate at least 3 hours or up to 3 days.

3. Combine powdered sugar, milk, corn syrup and remaining 1 teaspoon almond extract; stir until smooth. Cover; refrigerate up to 3 days.

4. Preheat oven to 375°F. Working with 1 disc of dough at a time, roll out on floured surface to ¼-inch thickness. Cut dough into desired shapes using 2½-inch cookie cutters. Place about 2 inches apart on ungreased cookie sheets. Bake 7 to 8 minutes or until edges are firm and bottoms are brown. Remove cookies to wire racks; cool completely.

5. Separate powdered sugar mixture into 3 or 4 batches in small bowls; tint each batch with desired food coloring. Frost cookies.

Baker's Tip: To freeze dough, place wrapped discs in resealable plastic food storage bags. Thaw at room temperature before using. Or, cut out dough; bake and cool cookies. Freeze unfrosted cookies up to 2 months. Thaw and frost as desired.

Choceur® Double Chocolate Cranberry Chunkies

Makes about 1 dozen large cookies

1½ bars (10.58 ounces each) Choceur® Austrian milk chocolate
1¾ cups Grandma's Best® all-purpose flour
⅓ cup Baker's Corner® baking cocoa
½ teaspoon Baker's Corner® baking powder
½ teaspoon Sebree® salt
1 cup (2 sticks) Happy Farms® butter, softened
1 cup Sweet Harvest® granulated sugar
½ cup packed Sweet Harvest® brown sugar
1 Goldhen® egg
1 teaspoon Spice Club® pure vanilla
¾ cup Fit & Active dried cranberries
  Additional Sweet Harvest® granulated sugar

1. Preheat oven to 350°F. Chop chocolate bars into small chunks to measure 2 cups; set aside. Use remaining chocolate for another use.

2. Combine flour, cocoa, baking powder and salt in small bowl; set aside. Beat butter, 1 cup granulated sugar and brown sugar in large bowl with electric mixer at medium speed until light and fluffy. Beat in egg and vanilla until well blended. Gradually beat in flour mixture at low speed until blended. Stir in chocolate chunks and cranberries.

3. Drop dough by level ¼ cupfuls onto ungreased cookie sheets 3 inches apart. Flatten dough to 2 inches in diameter with bottom of glass that has been dipped in additional granulated sugar.

4. Bake 11 to 12 minutes or until cookies are set. Cool cookies 2 minutes on cookie sheets. Remove to wire racks; cool completely.

Baker's Tip: For smaller cookies, drop by tablespoonfuls onto ungreased cookie sheets. Bake 8 to 10 minutes.

ALDI

Christmas Spritz Cookies

Makes about 5 dozen cookies

2¼ cups Grandma's Best® all-purpose flour
¼ teaspoon Sebree® salt
1¼ cups Sweet Harvest® powdered sugar
1 cup (2 sticks) Happy Farms® butter, softened
1 Goldhen® egg
1 teaspoon almond extract
1 teaspoon Spice Club® pure vanilla
Green food coloring (optional)
Icing (recipe follows, optional)
Assorted decorative candies

1. Preheat oven to 350°F. Combine flour and salt in medium bowl; set aside.

2. Beat powdered sugar and butter in large bowl with electric mixer at medium speed until light and fluffy. Beat in egg, almond extract and vanilla. Gradually add flour mixture. Beat until well blended.

3. Divide dough in half. Tint half of dough with green food coloring, if desired. Fit cookie press with desired plate (or change plates for different shapes after first batch). Fill press with dough; press dough 1 inch apart onto ungreased cookie sheets.

4. Bake 10 to 12 minutes or until just set. Remove cookies to wire racks; cool completely.

5. Prepare Icing, if desired. Pipe or drizzle on cooled cookies. Decorate as desired. Store tightly covered at room temperature or freeze up to 3 months.

Icing

1½ cups Sweet Harvest® powdered sugar
2 tablespoons Friendly Farms milk plus additional, if needed
⅛ teaspoon almond extract

Place all ingredients in medium bowl; stir until thick but spreadable. (If icing is too thick, stir in 1 teaspoon additional milk.)

13

Sweet Harvest® Icicle Ornaments

Makes about 2¹/₂ dozen cookies

2½ cups Grandma's Best® all-purpose flour
¼ teaspoon Sebree® salt
1 cup Sweet Harvest® granulated sugar
¾ cup (1½ sticks) Happy Farms® butter, softened
8 to 10 rectangles (about 2 ounces) Choceur® white chocolate, melted
1 Goldhen® egg
1 teaspoon Spice Club® pure vanilla
Coarse white decorating sugar, colored sugars and decors
Ribbon

1. Combine flour and salt in medium bowl. Beat sugar and butter in large bowl with electric mixer at medium speed until fluffy. Beat in white chocolate, egg and vanilla. Gradually add flour mixture. Beat at low speed until well blended. Shape dough into disc. Wrap tightly in Kwik-N-Fresh® plastic wrap; refrigerate 30 minutes or until firm.

2. Preheat oven to 350°F. Spray cookie sheets with Ariel® no stick cooking spray. Shape heaping tablespoonfuls of dough into 10-inch ropes. Fold each rope in half; twist to make icicle shape, leaving opening at fold and tapering ends. Roll in coarse sugar; sprinkle with colored sugars and decors as desired. Place 1 inch apart on prepared cookie sheets.

3. Bake 8 to 10 minutes or until firm but not browned. Cool on cookie sheets 1 minute. Remove to wire racks; cool completely. Pull ribbon through opening in top of each icicle; tie small knot in ribbon ends.

Baker's Tip: Finely chop white or milk chocolate so that it melts quickly. Melt chocolate slowly over low heat. If chocolate gets too hot, it scorches or becomes gritty.

Shop at **ALDI**®

*Kids love decorating cookies. Prepare for a cookie decorating party with quality **ALDI**® ingredients. Combine powdered sugar and milk to make glazes or frostings. Melt white and milk chocolate bars to drizzle over cookies with a spoon or fork. Tint coconut by diluting a few drops of liquid food coloring with ¹/₂ teaspoon of milk or water. Add to 1 cup coconut and toss with a fork until the coconut is evenly tinted. Use colorful small candies for extra color. You're ready for fun and festive decorating.*

La Mas Rica
Mexican Wedding Cookies

Makes about 4 dozen cookies

1 cup Southern Grove® pecans
1 cup (2 sticks) Happy Farms® butter, softened
2 cups Sweet Harvest® powdered sugar, divided
2 teaspoons Spice Club® pure vanilla
2 cups Grandma's Best® all-purpose flour, divided
⅛ teaspoon Sebree® salt

1. Place pecans in food processor. Process using on/off pulses until pecans are ground but not pasty.

2. Beat butter, ½ cup powdered sugar and vanilla in large bowl with electric mixer at medium speed until light and fluffy. Gradually add 1 cup flour and salt. Beat at low speed until well blended. Stir in remaining 1 cup flour and ground nuts with spoon. Shape dough into ball. Wrap in Kwik-N-Fresh® plastic wrap; refrigerate 1 hour or until firm.

3. Preheat oven to 350°F. Shape dough into 1-inch balls. Place 1 inch apart on ungreased cookie sheets. Bake 12 to 15 minutes or until golden brown. Let cookies stand on cookie sheets 2 minutes.

4. Meanwhile, place 1 cup powdered sugar in 13×9-inch glass dish. Transfer hot cookies to powdered sugar. Roll cookies in powdered sugar, coating well. Let cookies cool in sugar.

5. Sift remaining ½ cup powdered sugar over sugar-coated cookies before serving. Store tightly covered at room temperature, or freeze up to 1 month.

16

ALDI

Berryhill® Golden Kolacky

Makes about 2¹/₂ dozen cookies

½ cup (1 stick) Happy Farms® butter, softened
4 ounces Happy Farms® cream cheese, softened
1 cup Grandma's Best® all-purpose flour
   Berryhill® fruit preserves

1. Beat butter and cream cheese in large bowl with electric mixer at medium speed until smooth and fluffy. Gradually add flour; beat at low speed until mixture forms soft dough. Divide dough in half; wrap each half in Kwik-N-Fresh® plastic wrap. Refrigerate about 1 hour or until firm.

2. Preheat oven to 375°F. Roll out dough, half at a time, on floured surface to ¹/₈-inch thickness. Cut into 2¹/₂-inch squares. Spoon 1 teaspoon preserves into center of each square. Bring up two opposite corners to center; pinch together tightly to seal. Fold sealed tip to one side; pinch to seal. Place 1 inch apart on ungreased cookie sheets. Bake 10 to 13 minutes or until lightly browned. Remove to wire racks; cool completely.

Save at **ALDI**®
The Baker's Pantry

*Ring in the season with festive homemade goodies and impressive desserts. Start by filling your pantry with ingredients that are most commonly used in baking recipes. Stock up on top quality ingredients from **ALDI**®—your one-stop shop for holiday baking.*

Baking powder	Corn syrup	Quick oatmeal
Baking soda	Cream cheese	Raisins
Baking cocoa	Dried cranberries	Shortening
Butter	Eggs	Sugar
Chocolate bars (white & milk chocolate)	Flour (all-purpose)	(brown, granulated and powdered)
	Milk	
Chocolate chips (semisweet & white)	Nuts (almonds, pecans, walnuts)	Sweetened condensed milk
Coconut		Vanilla
	Peanut butter	Vegetable oil

ALDI

Gingerbread Bears

Makes about 3½ dozen cookies

3½ cups Grandma's Best® all-purpose flour
2 teaspoons ground cinnamon
1½ teaspoons ground ginger
1 teaspoon Sebree® salt
1 teaspoon Baker's Corner® baking soda
1 teaspoon ground allspice
1 cup (2 sticks) Happy Farms® butter, softened
1 cup packed Sweet Harvest® light brown sugar
1 teaspoon Spice Club® pure vanilla
⅓ cup molasses
2 Goldhen® eggs
Ornamental Frosting (page 21)
Assorted nonpareils, colored sugars and assorted candies (optional)

1. Combine flour, cinnamon, ginger, salt, baking soda and allspice in medium bowl. Beat butter, brown sugar and vanilla in large bowl with electric mixer at medium speed until light and fluffy. Beat in molasses and eggs until well blended. Beat in flour mixture at low speed until well blended. Shape dough into 3 equal discs. Tightly wrap each disc in Kwik-N-Fresh® plastic wrap; refrigerate at least 2 hours or up to 24 hours.

2. Preheat oven to 350°F. Spray large cookie sheets with Ariel® no stick cooking spray.

3. Working with 1 portion at a time, roll dough on lightly floured surface to ⅛-inch thickness. Cut dough with 3-inch bear-shaped cookie cutter. Place cutouts 1 inch apart on prepared cookie sheets. Shape dough scraps into small balls and ropes to make noses and ears.

4. Bake 10 minutes or until edges are lightly browned. Cool cookies on cookie sheets 1 minute. Remove to wire racks; cool completely.

5. Prepare Ornamental Frosting, if desired. Pipe or spread frosting on cooled cookies; decorate as desired. Store tightly covered at room temperature.

Ornamental Frosting

Makes about 2 cups

½ cup (1 stick) Happy Farms® butter, softened
1 teaspoon Spice Club® pure vanilla
4 cups (16 ounces) sifted Sweet Harvest® powdered sugar
2 tablespoons Friendly Farms milk

Beat butter and vanilla in large bowl with electric mixer at medium speed. Beat in powdered sugar and enough milk at low speed until frosting is of desired spreading consistency.

Cocoa Crinkle Sandwiches

Makes about 20 sandwich cookies

1¾ cups Grandma's Best® all-purpose flour

½ cup Baker's Corner® baking cocoa

1 teaspoon Baker's Corner® baking soda

¼ teaspoon Sebree® salt

½ cup (1 stick) Happy Farms® butter

2¼ cups Sweet Harvest® granulated sugar, divided

2 Goldhen® eggs

2 teaspoons Spice Club® pure vanilla

1 container (16 ounces) Baker's Corner® chocolate frosting

½ cup crushed Mystik® Starlite mints* or candy canes

*To crush mints, place candy in resealable heavy-duty plastic food storage bag; seal. Break into pieces with heavy object such as meat mallet or can of vegetables; crush pieces with rolling pin.

1. Combine flour, cocoa, baking soda and salt in medium bowl. Melt butter in large saucepan over medium heat; cool slightly. Add 1¾ cups sugar; whisk until smooth. Whisk in eggs, 1 at a time, until well blended. Stir in vanilla until smooth. Stir in flour mixture just until blended. Shape dough into disc. Tightly wrap dough in Kwik-N-Fresh® plastic wrap; refrigerate 2 hours.

2. Preheat oven to 350°F. Grease cookie sheets with Carlini® vegetable shortening. Shape dough into 1-inch balls. Place remaining ½ cup sugar in shallow bowl; roll balls in sugar. Place 1½ inches apart on prepared cookie sheets. Bake 12 minutes or until set. Cool cookies on cookie sheets 5 minutes. Remove to wire racks; cool completely.

3. Stir frosting until soft and smooth. Place crushed mints on piece of waxed paper. Spread about 2 teaspoons frosting over flat side of one cookie. Place second cookie, flat side down, over frosting, pressing down to allow frosting to squeeze out slightly between cookies. Press exposed frosting into crushed mints. Repeat with remaining cookies, frosting and mints. Store in airtight container.

Baker's Tip: For added mint flavor, add ½ teaspoon peppermint extract to the frosting.

Moravian Spice Crisps

Makes about 6 dozen cookies

⅓ cup Carlini® vegetable shortening
⅓ cup packed Sweet Harvest® light brown sugar
¼ cup molasses
¼ cup Baker's Corner® corn syrup
1¾ to 2 cups Grandma's Best® all-purpose flour, divided
2 teaspoons ground ginger
1¼ teaspoons Baker's Corner® baking soda
1 teaspoon ground cinnamon
½ teaspoon ground cloves
Sweet Harvest® powdered sugar

1. Melt shortening in small saucepan over low heat. Remove from heat; stir in brown sugar, molasses and corn syrup. Set aside to cool.

2. Combine 1½ cups flour, ginger, baking soda, cinnamon and cloves in large bowl. Beat in shortening mixture. Gradually beat in remaining ¼ cup flour to form stiff dough. Knead dough on lightly floured surface, adding more flour if dough is too sticky. Shape dough into 2 equal discs. Tightly wrap in Kwik-N-Fresh® plastic wrap; refrigerate 30 minutes or until firm.

3. Preheat oven to 350°F. Spray cookie sheets with Ariel® no stick cooking spray. Working with 1 disc at a time, roll out dough on lightly floured surface to ¹⁄₁₆-inch thickness. Cut dough with floured 2¼-inch cookie cutter. (If dough becomes too soft, refrigerate several minutes before continuing.) Gently press dough trimmings together; reroll and cut out more cookies. Place cutouts ½ inch apart on prepared cookie sheets.

4. Bake 8 minutes or until firm and lightly browned. Remove cookies to wire racks; cool completely. Place small strips of cardboard or parchment paper over cookies; dust with sifted powdered sugar. Carefully remove cardboard.

Baker's Tip: Place a paper doily over the cookies, then dust with powdered sugar to create different patterns.

Viennese Almond Butter Thins

Makes about 3 dozen cookies

1 cup Southern Grove® almonds, toasted* or hazelnuts
1¼ cups Grandma's Best® all-purpose flour
¼ teaspoon Sebree® salt
1¼ cups Sweet Harvest® powdered sugar
1 cup (2 sticks) Happy Farms® butter, softened
1 Goldhen® egg
1 teaspoon Spice Club® pure vanilla
1 bar (10.58 ounces) Choceur® Austrian milk chocolate

To toast almonds, spread in single layer on baking sheet. Bake in preheated 350°F oven 8 to 10 minutes or until golden brown, stirring frequently.

1. Preheat oven to 350°F. Wrap nuts in heavy kitchen towel; rub against towel to remove as much of the skins as possible. Place nuts in food processor. Process using on/off pulses until nuts are ground but not pasty.

2. Combine flour and salt in small bowl. Beat powdered sugar and butter in large bowl with electric mixer at medium speed until light and fluffy. Beat in egg and vanilla. Gradually add flour mixture. Beat in ground nuts at low speed until well blended. (Dough will be very sticky.)

3. Place dough on sheet of waxed paper. Using waxed paper to hold dough, roll back and forth to form 12×2½-inch log. Wrap log in Kwik-N-Fresh® plastic wrap. Refrigerate at least 2 hours or up to 48 hours until firm.

4. Preheat oven to 350°F. Cut dough into ¼-inch-thick slices; place on ungreased cookie sheets. Bake 10 to 12 minutes or until edges are very lightly browned. Cool cookies on cookie sheets 1 minute. Remove to wire racks; cool completely.

5. Chop chocolate bar into small pieces; place in 2-cup glass measure. Microwave at HIGH 1 minute or until melted.

6. Dip cookies into chocolate, coating about half of each cookie; let excess drip back into cup. Or, spread chocolate on cookies with a narrow spatula. Place cookies on sheets of Kwik-N-Fresh® aluminum foil; let stand at room temperature 1 hour or until set.

Baker's Tip: To store cookies, place in airtight container between layers of waxed paper. Cookies can be frozen for up to 3 months.

ALDI

Crispy Thumbprint Cookies

Makes 3 dozen cookies

1 package (18.5 ounces) Baker's Corner® yellow cake mix
½ cup Carlini® vegetable oil
¼ cup water
1 Goldhen® egg
3 cups Millville® crisp rice cereal, crushed
½ cup chopped Southern Grove® walnuts
6 tablespoons Berryhill® strawberry or raspberry preserves

1. Preheat oven to 375°F.

2. Combine cake mix, oil, water and egg in large bowl. Beat with electric mixer at medium speed until well blended. Stir in cereal and walnuts; mix well.

3. Drop dough by heaping teaspoonfuls about 2 inches apart onto ungreased cookie sheets. Use thumb to make indentation in each cookie. Spoon about ¹/₂ teaspoon preserves into center of each cookie.

4. Bake 9 to 11 minutes or until golden brown. Cool cookies 1 minute on cookie sheets. Remove to wire racks; cool completely.

ALDI

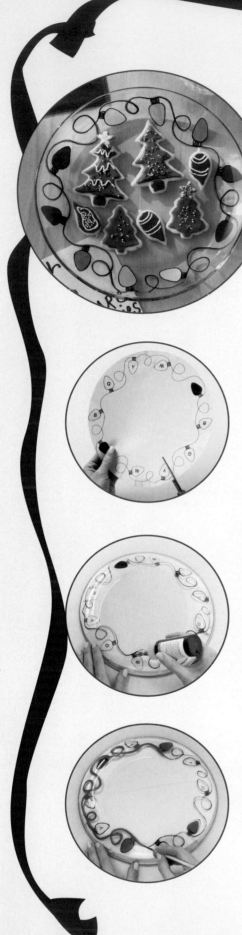

Bright Lights Cookie Plate

WHAT YOU'LL NEED
- **Pattern on page 31**
- **Scissors**
- **Masking tape**
- **Ruler**
- **Clear, smooth 10-inch glass plate**
- **Bottle-tip nozzle pen set**
- **Enamel paint: black, green, white, yellow, red, and blue**
- **Foam plate**
- **#2 round paintbrushes**

1. Use copier to make 2 copies of bulb pattern. Cut out patterns along semicircle outline. Flip 1 pattern so ends of cord outline match up with other pattern, creating a continuous circular pattern. Tape in place. Snip ½-inch tabs all around pattern to allow paper to conform to plate. Position and tape pattern face down on top of glass plate. Design will be painted on bottom of plate.

2. Using pen set, attach extension cap and fine metal tip to black enamel bottle. Practice squeezing lines of enamel from bottle onto foam plate, then draw thin black definition lines on glass plate for sockets and cords and around each bulb. Let dry. (Quickly and thoroughly rinse out cap and metal tip after each use.)

3. Thin small amount of green enamel with water on foam plate. Using pattern as your guide and painting on top of black definition lines, paint a line over coiling cord. Also use green to fill in sockets and 2 green bulbs. Be sure to apply paint strokes in same direction. Let dry, and repeat if necessary to achieve opaque coverage.

4. Thin small amount of white enamel with water, and paint white light bulbs. Repeat with remaining paint colors to fill in yellow, red, and blue bulbs.

5. Follow manufacturer's instructions on enamel bottles for drying, baking, and curing enamel to glass.

Tip: *Painting mistakes can be easily removed by washing them away with water before the paint has dried completely or by scraping the dried enamel off with your fingernail. Remember: Once the enamel has been cured, it becomes permanent.*

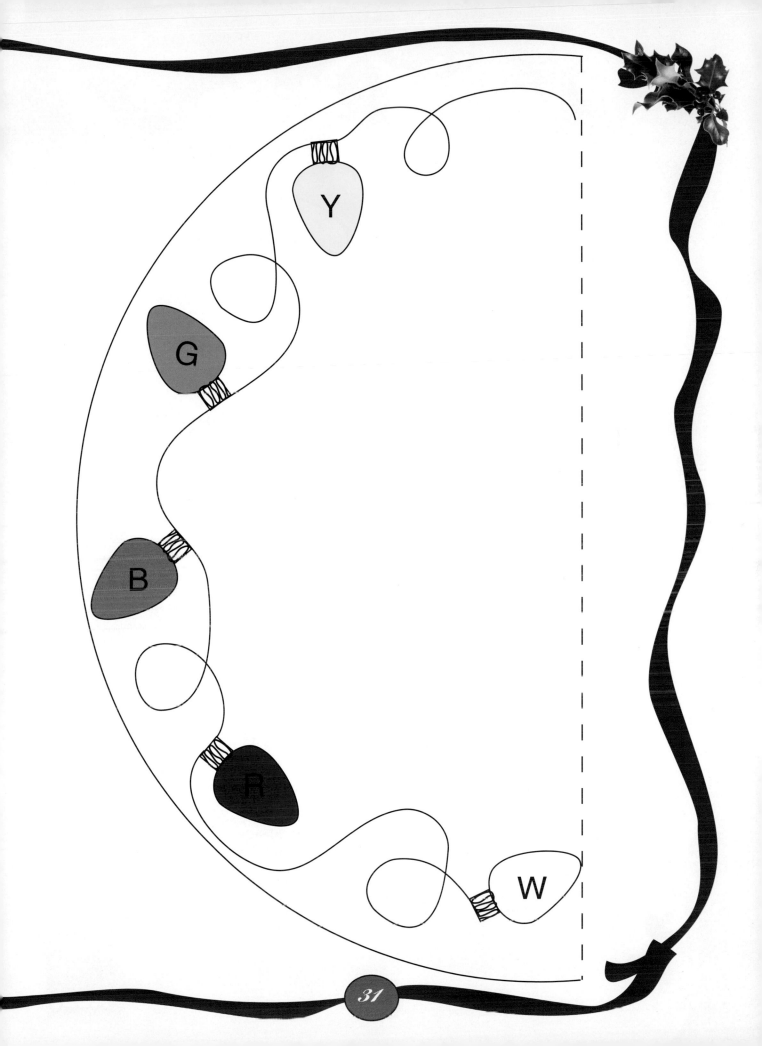

CHAPTER 2

Merry Bars

Baker's Corner®
Coconut, Cherry & White Chocolate Bars

Makes about 2 dozen bars

2 cups Grandma's Best® all-purpose flour
1 teaspoon Baker's Corner® baking soda
½ teaspoon Sebree® salt
1 cup (2 sticks) Happy Farms® butter, softened
¾ cup Sweet Harvest® granulated sugar
¾ cup packed Sweet Harvest® light brown sugar
2 Goldhen® eggs
1 teaspoon Spice Club® pure vanilla
1 cup Millville® quick oats
2 cups Baker's Corner® white chocolate chips, divided
1 cup Baker's Corner® coconut flakes
¾ cup dried cherries or cherry-flavored dried cranberries

1. Preheat oven to 375°F. Spray 15×10-inch jelly-roll pan with Ariel® no stick cooking spray.

2. Combine flour, baking soda and salt in medium bowl; mix well. Beat butter and sugars in large bowl with electric mixer at medium speed until creamy. Add eggs and vanilla; beat until blended. Gradually add flour mixture. Beat at low speed until blended. Add oats; beat until blended. Add 1½ cups white chocolate chips, coconut and cherries; stir just until well blended.

3. Press dough evenly into prepared pan. Sprinkle top with remaining ½ cup white chocolate chips. Bake 16 to 18 minutes or until edges are golden brown and center is almost set. Cool completely in pan on wire rack. Cut into bars or diamond shapes.

33

Sweet Harvest® Pumpkin Brownies

Makes 9 brownies

1 cup (2 sticks) Happy Farms® butter, softened
¾ cup packed Sweet Harvest® light brown sugar
1 teaspoon Spice Club® pure vanilla
1 Goldhen® egg
1⅓ cups Grandma's Best® all-purpose flour
1 cup Sweet Harvest® solid-pack pumpkin
2 teaspoons pumpkin pie spice
1 teaspoon Baker's Corner® baking powder
¼ teaspoon Sebree® salt
½ cup toffee baking bits
White Chocolate Cream Cheese Frosting (recipe follows)

1. Preheat oven to 350°F. Spray 8-inch square baking pan with Ariel® no stick cooking spray.

2. Beat butter, brown sugar and vanilla in large bowl with electric mixer at medium speed until smooth. Add egg; beat until fluffy. Stir in flour, pumpkin, pumpkin pie spice, baking powder and salt. Fold in toffee bits. Spread evenly in prepared pan.

3. Bake 40 to 45 minutes or until toothpick inserted near center comes out clean. Cool completely in pan on wire rack. Meanwhile, prepare White Chocolate Cream Cheese Frosting. Frost brownies; cut into squares.

White Chocolate Cream Cheese Frosting

Makes about 2 cups frosting

2 tablespoons whipping cream
8 rectangles (4 ounces) Choceur® white chocolate, chopped
6 ounces Happy Farms® cream cheese, softened
⅓ cup Sweet Harvest® powdered sugar, sifted

Heat cream in small saucepan over medium heat until almost boiling; remove from heat. Add white chocolate; stir until completely melted. Cool slightly. Beat cream cheese and sugar in large bowl with electric mixer at medium speed 1 minute or until fluffy. Add chocolate mixture; beat until smooth.

Merry Cherry Sour Cream Bars

Makes about 2 dozen bars

2½ cups Grandma's Best® all-purpose flour
2 teaspoons ground cinnamon
1 teaspoon Baker's Corner® baking soda
½ teaspoon Sebree® salt
½ teaspoon ground allspice
1½ cups packed Sweet Harvest® light brown sugar
1 cup (2 sticks) Happy Farms® butter
¾ cup Friendly Farms sour cream
2 Goldhen® eggs
1 teaspoon Spice Club® pure vanilla
1½ cups dried cherries or cherry-flavored cranberries

FROSTING
1 package (8 ounces) Happy Farms® cream cheese, chilled
¼ cup (½ stick) Happy Farms® butter, softened
2 to 2½ cups Sweet Harvest® powdered sugar
1 teaspoon Spice Club® pure vanilla

ALDI

1. Preheat oven to 350°F. Spray 13×9-inch baking pan with Ariel® no stick cooking spray. Combine flour, cinnamon, baking soda, salt and allspice in medium bowl.

2. Beat brown sugar and butter in large bowl with electric mixer at medium speed until fluffy. Add sour cream, eggs and vanilla; beat until well blended. Gradually add flour mixture to butter mixture beating at low speed until well blended. Stir in cherries. Spread mixture evenly into prepared pan. Bake 25 to 30 minutes or until golden brown. Cool completely on wire rack.

3. For frosting, cut cream cheese and butter into chunks and place in bowl of food processor fitted with steel blade. Add 2 cups powdered sugar and vanilla. Process using on/off pulses just until well blended. *(Do not over process or frosting will become thin.)* If frosting is too stiff, process 10 seconds longer. If frosting is too soft, add additional powdered sugar as needed. Spread frosting evenly over cooled cookies. Chill until frosting is set, about 50 minutes. Cut into bars, squares or diamonds.

Baker's Tip: When in a hurry, frost the cookies with prepared Baker's Corner® cream cheese or vanilla frosting.

Multiloop Bow

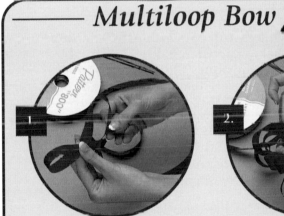  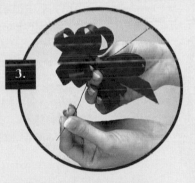

1. Unroll several yards of ribbon from bolt. Form ribbon loops with your dominant hand. Hold center of loops tightly with thumb and forefinger of your other hand as you work.

2. Continue to add loops to bow. Keep pinching bow's center with your thumb and forefinger. After you have all the loops you desire, cut ribbon from the bolt. If you want a streamer, leave ribbon longer before cutting.

3. Insert length of wire through center of ribbon. Bring 2 wire ends securely next to bow's center to eliminate loop slippage. Attach bow with wire or trim wire and glue bow in place.

German Honey Bars (Lebkuchen)

Makes about 6 dozen bars

2¾ cups Grandma's Best® all-purpose flour
2 teaspoons ground cinnamon
1 teaspoon Baker's Corner® baking powder
½ teaspoon Baker's Corner® baking soda
½ teaspoon Sebree® salt
½ teaspoon ground cardamom
½ teaspoon ground ginger
½ cup Golden Nectar® honey
½ cup dark molasses
¾ cup packed Sweet Harvest® light brown sugar
3 tablespoons Happy Farms® butter, melted
1 Goldhen® egg
½ cup chopped toasted Southern Grove® almonds*
Glaze (recipe follows)

To toast almonds, spread in single layer on baking sheet. Bake in preheated 350°F oven 8 to 10 minutes or until golden brown, stirring frequently.

1. Preheat oven to 350°F. Spray 15×10-inch jelly-roll pan with Ariel® no stick cooking spray. Combine flour, cinnamon, baking powder, baking soda, salt, cardamom and ginger in medium bowl. Combine honey and molasses in medium saucepan; bring to a boil over medium heat. Remove from heat; cool 10 minutes. Stir in brown sugar, butter and egg.

2. Place brown sugar mixture in large bowl. Gradually add flour mixture. Beat with electric mixer at low speed until dough forms. Stir in almonds. (Dough will be slightly sticky.) Spread dough evenly into prepared pan. Bake 20 to 22 minutes or until golden brown. Cool completely in pan on wire rack.

3. Prepare Glaze. Spread over cooled cookies. Let stand until set, about 30 minutes. Cut into 2×1-inch bars. Store tightly covered at room temperature, or freeze up to 3 months.

Glaze

1¼ cups Sweet Harvest® powdered sugar
1 teaspoon grated lemon peel
3 tablespoons fresh lemon juice

Combine all ingredients in medium bowl; stir until smooth.

Ornament Brownies

Makes about 8 brownies

1 cup (6 ounces) Baker's Corner® real semisweet chocolate chips
1 tablespoon Beaumont® instant coffee granules
1 tablespoon boiling water
¾ cup Grandma's Best® all-purpose flour
¾ teaspoon ground cinnamon
½ teaspoon Baker's Corner® baking powder
¼ teaspoon Sebree® salt
½ cup Sweet Harvest® granulated sugar
¼ cup (½ stick) Happy Farms® butter, softened
2 Goldhen® eggs
Baker's Corner® vanilla frosting
Assorted food colorings
Small candy canes, assorted candies and sprinkles

1. Preheat oven to 350°F. Spray 8-inch square baking pan with Ariel® no stick cooking spray; set aside. Melt chocolate in small heavy saucepan over low heat, stirring constantly; set aside. Dissolve coffee granules in boiling water in small cup; set aside. Combine flour, cinnamon, baking powder and salt in small bowl.

2. Beat sugar and butter in large bowl with electric mixer at medium speed until light and fluffy. Beat in eggs, 1 at a time. Beat in melted chocolate and coffee until well combined. Add flour mixture. Beat at low speed until well blended. Spread batter evenly in prepared pan. Bake 30 to 35 minutes or until center is set. Cool completely in pan on wire rack. Cut into holiday shapes using 2-inch cookie cutters.

3. Tint frosting with food colorings. Frost brownies. Break off top of small candy cane to create loop. Insert in top of brownie. Decorate as desired.

Sweet Harvest® Buried Cherry Bars

Makes 24 bars

1 jar (10 ounces) Sweet Harvest® maraschino cherries
1 package (18.5 ounces) Baker's Corner® Devil's Food cake mix
1 cup (2 sticks) Happy Farms® butter, melted
1 Goldhen® egg
½ teaspoon almond extract
1½ cups Baker's Corner® real semisweet chocolate chips
¾ cup Friendly Farms sweetened condensed milk
½ cup chopped Southern Grove® pecans

1. Preheat oven to 350°F. Spray 13×9-inch baking pan with Ariel® no stick cooking spray. Drain maraschino cherries; reserve 3 tablespoons juice. Cut cherries into quarters.

2. Combine cake mix, butter, egg and almond extract in large bowl; mix well. (Batter will be very thick.) Spread batter in prepared pan. Lightly press cherries into batter.

3. Combine chocolate chips and sweetened condensed milk in small saucepan. Cook over low heat, stirring constantly, until chocolate melts. Stir in reserved cherry juice. Spread chocolate mixture over cherries in pan; sprinkle with pecans.

4. Bake 35 minutes or until almost set in center. Cool completely in pan on wire rack.

ALDI

Cranberry-Lime Squares

Makes 35 squares

2¼ cups Grandma's Best® all-purpose flour, divided

½ cup Sweet Harvest® powdered sugar

1 tablespoon plus 1 teaspoon grated lime peel, divided

¼ teaspoon Sebree® salt

1 cup (2 sticks) Happy Farms® butter

2 cups Sweet Harvest® granulated sugar

1 teaspoon Baker's Corner® baking powder

4 Goldhen® eggs

¼ cup lime juice (about 1½ limes)

1 cup Fit & Active dried cranberries

Additional Sweet Harvest® powdered sugar

1. Preheat oven to 350°F. Spray 13×9-inch baking pan with Ariel® no stick cooking spray.

2. Combine 2 cups flour, powdered sugar, 1 tablespoon lime peel and salt in large bowl. Cut in butter with pastry blender or two knives until mixture forms coarse crumbs. Press mixture evenly into prepared baking pan. Bake 18 to 20 minutes or until golden brown.

3. Meanwhile, combine remaining ¼ cup flour, granulated sugar and baking powder in bowl; mix well. Combine eggs and lime juice in separate large bowl. Add flour mixture to egg mixture; beat with electric mixer at medium speed until well blended. Stir in remaining 1 teaspoon lime peel and cranberries. Pour over warm crust.

4. Bake 20 to 25 minutes until golden brown and set. Cool completely in pan on wire rack. Sprinkle with powdered sugar; chill 2 hours. Cut into squares. Serve chilled.

Chocolate Caramel Pecan Bars

Makes 40 bars

2 cups (4 sticks) Happy Farms® butter, softened, divided
½ cup Sweet Harvest® granulated sugar, divided
1 Goldhen® egg
2¾ cups Grandma's Best® all-purpose flour
⅔ cup packed Sweet Harvest® light brown sugar
¼ cup Baker's Corner® light corn syrup
2½ cups coarsely chopped Southern Grove® pecans
1 cup Baker's Corner® real semisweet chocolate chips

1. Preheat oven to 375°F. Spray 15×10-inch jelly-roll pan with Ariel® no stick cooking spray.

2. Beat 1 cup butter and granulated sugar in large bowl with electric mixer at medium speed until light and fluffy. Beat in egg. Add flour. Beat at low speed until just blended. Spread dough in prepared pan. Bake 20 minutes or until light golden brown.

3. Meanwhile, combine remaining 1 cup butter, brown sugar and corn syrup in medium heavy saucepan. Bring to a boil over medium heat, stirring frequently. Boil 2 minutes without stirring. Quickly stir in pecans; spread over crust. Bake 20 minutes or until dark golden brown and bubbling.

4. Immediately sprinkle chocolate chips evenly over hot caramel mixture. Gently press chips into caramel topping with spatula. Cool completely in pan on wire rack. Cut into 3×1½-inch bars. Store tightly covered at room temperature, or freeze up to 3 months.

December

ALDI® tips for a Memorable and Merry Christmas

4

5

Mail packages

Don't wait till the last minute. Avoid expensive shipping charges and long lines by mailing early. Homebaked treats like Friendly Farms® Cherry Eggnog Quick Bread (page 50) make thoughtful gifts. Just mark the package, "Open and enjoy before the holidays."

6

7

Make holiday stationery

Get the kids together to make Snowy Stationery (page 60). It will lend a warm personal touch to letters to Santa, holiday newsletters, party invitations and much more.

11

Shop for gifts

When you're tired of the crowds at the mall, remember that **ALDI®** gift certificates are perfect for almost everyone on your list. Also check **ALDI®** Special Purchase items at www.ALDI.com for gift ideas that are also a great value.

12

13

14

Finish decorating

Do some last minute decorating. Don't forget to hang the stocking, display the holiday cards you've received and arrange those special candles and table decorations. Then relax with the family and sip some hot mulled cider.

18

Make the grocery list

It's time to put together menus and grocery lists for all your holiday entertaining. Be sure to stock extra goodies for last minute visitors and don't forget that **ALDI®** has an excellent selection of affordable wines.

19

20

21

Merry Christmas

25

Store the leftovers

ALDI® Kwik-N-Fresh® plastic storage containers will keep delicious leftovers fresh for easy meals and snacks all week long. Who has the time to cook when there's so much to celebrate?

26

Let's go sledding

Plan a holiday family outing such as sledding or skating to enjoy the nip in the air. Be sure to have LaMissa® Hot Cocoa Mix on hand to warm you up when you come in from the winter weather.

27

28

Shop at ALDI® for New Year's celebrations!

From champagne to mixed nuts, **ALDI®** has everything you'll need for a happy new year. You can pick up chips, dips, pizza and ready-to-serve snacks so you can spend more time having fun.

29

30

31

Happy New Y

Send holiday cards

Make sending cards a family activity instead of a chore. Play holiday music and enlist the kids to help lick the envelopes and stick the stamps. Including a family photo with your card makes faraway friends feel closer.

1

2

Decorate with a wreath!

What could be more festive than a holiday wreath? Create an edible homemade Holiday Candy Wreath (page 76) and you'll have a beautiful decoration and a delicious treat.

3

8

Stock your pantry

Let the baking begin! Check the list on page 18 for suggestions and pick up everything you'll need for the baking season at **ALDI**®.

9

It's snowflake day!

Time to stir up a batch of Buttery Almond Cutouts (page 8). A snowflake cookie cutter and some ready-to-spread frosting from **ALDI**® make it quick and easy. Ask the kids to cut out paper snowflakes for decorations while the cookies bake.

10

Buy poinsettias

Fill your house with the holiday spirit by purchasing poinsettias in a variety of sizes and colors. Place them throughout the house (don't forget the powder room!), but remember to keep them out of reach of small children and pets.

15

16

Plan a family baking day

Nothing captures the warmth of the season like a homemade gift. Get out the cookie cutters and baking pans. Pack finished products in decorative tins or boxes as a gift for teachers, bus drivers, mail carriers and friends.

17

Buy stocking stuffers

Choceur® chocolate bars and other holiday sweets from **ALDI**® make excellent stocking stuffers or grab-bag gifts. Special teas and coffees are also great last minute gifts. Remember to get a special treat for your pets, too.

22

Final preparations

It's almost here! Finish wrapping the presents and get out the special dishes and ornaments. Create a family tradition to share. Go caroling, take a drive to look at holiday decorations or just watch your favorite holiday movie together.

23

Homemade cookies for Santa

Santa likes all kinds of cookies, but we've heard that Festive Fudge Blossoms (page 6) are his favorites. Have the kids help you bake a batch and set them out along with a big glass of milk where Santa will be sure to find them.

24

CHAPTER 3

Festive Breads

Friendly Farms®
Cherry Eggnog Quick Bread

Makes 3 mini loaves

2½ cups Grandma's Best® all-purpose flour

¾ cup Sweet Harvest® granulated sugar

1 tablespoon Baker's Corner® baking powder

½ teaspoon ground nutmeg

1¼ cups Friendly Farms dairy eggnog
  or half-and-half

½ cup (1 stick) Happy Farms® butter,
  melted and cooled

2 Goldhen® eggs, lightly beaten

1 teaspoon Spice Club® pure vanilla

½ cup chopped Southern Grove® pecans

½ cup coarsely chopped candied red cherries

1. Preheat oven to 350°F. Spray three 5½×3-inch mini-loaf pans with Ariel®
no stick cooking spray.

2. Combine flour, sugar, baking powder and nutmeg in large bowl. Combine
eggnog, butter, eggs and vanilla in medium bowl; stir until well blended. Add
eggnog mixture to flour mixture. Mix just until all ingredients are moistened.
Stir in pecans and cherries. Spoon into prepared pans.

3. Bake 35 to 40 minutes or until wooden toothpick inserted into centers
comes out clean. Cool in pans 15 minutes. Remove from pans; cool
completely on wire racks. Store tightly wrapped in Kwik-N-Fresh® plastic
wrap at room temperature.

Peanut Delight®
Peanut Butter Bread

Makes 1 loaf

¾ cup packed Sweet Harvest® light brown sugar
½ cup Peanut Delight® peanut butter
½ cup (1 stick) Happy Farms® butter, cut into 3 pieces
2 Goldhen® eggs
1 cup Grandma's Best® all-purpose flour
½ cup whole wheat flour
2 teaspoons Baker's Corner® baking powder
½ teaspoon ground cinnamon
¼ teaspoon Sebree® salt
¼ teaspoon Baker's Corner® baking soda
¼ teaspoon ground nutmeg
¼ teaspoon ground allspice
⅔ cup Friendly Farms milk
½ teaspoon Spice Club® pure vanilla
1 cup chopped Southern Grove® dry roasted peanuts
Creamy Ginger Spread (page 53)

1. Preheat oven to 325°F. Spray 8½×4½×2½-inch loaf pan with Ariel® no stick cooking spray.

2. Fit food processor with steel blade. Place sugar, peanut butter and butter into work bowl. Process until smooth, about 10 seconds. Add eggs; process until well blended. Add flours, baking powder, cinnamon, salt, baking soda, nutmeg and allspice. Process on/off pulses to mix.

3. Pour milk and vanilla over flour mixture. Process just until flour is moistened. Do not overprocess. Batter should be lumpy. Sprinkle peanuts over batter. Process on/off pulses until peanuts are just mixed into batter.

4. Pour batter into prepared pan. Bake 1 hour or until toothpick inserted into center comes out clean. Cool bread in pan on wire rack 15 minutes. Remove from pan; cool completely on wire rack. Serve with Creamy Ginger Spread.

Creamy Ginger Spread

Makes about ²/₃ cup

3 ounces Happy Farms® cream cheese, softened
2 tablespoons Happy Farms® butter
2 tablespoons Golden Nectar® honey
⅛ teaspoon ground ginger

Fit food processor with steel blade. Place all ingredients in work bowl. Process 20 to 30 seconds or until well blended.

Cherry, Almond & Chocolate Breakfast Wreath

Makes 1 wreath

1 cup dried sweet or sour cherries
½ cup Sweet Harvest® granulated sugar, divided
¼ cup warm water (105° to 115°F)
1 package active dry yeast
½ cup plus 1 tablespoon Friendly Farms milk, divided
3 tablespoons Happy Farms® butter, cut into pieces
2 Goldhen® eggs, divided
1 tablespoon grated lemon peel
½ teaspoon Sebree® salt
½ teaspoon almond extract
2¼ to 2¾ cups Grandma's Best® all-purpose flour
1¼ cups canned almond filling (about 12 ounces)
¾ cup Baker's Corner® real semisweet chocolate chips
Almond Glaze (page 56)

1. Spray large bowl with Ariel® no stick cooking spray. Combine *1 cup water,* cherries and ¼ cup sugar in small saucepan. Bring to a boil over high heat, stirring constantly. Remove from heat. Cover; set aside.

2. Place ¼ cup warm water in separate large bowl. Sprinkle yeast over water. Let stand 5 minutes. Stir to dissolve.

3. Meanwhile heat ½ cup milk and butter in medium saucepan over high heat until milk bubbles around edge of saucepan, stirring constantly (butter does not need to melt completely). Remove saucepan from heat; stir occasionally until milk is warm to touch.

4. Add milk mixture to yeast mixture. Stir in remaining ¼ cup sugar, 1 egg, lemon peel, salt and almond extract until well blended. Add 2¼ cups flour; stir until dough forms sticky ball. Stir in enough remaining flour until soft dough forms.

5. Place dough on lightly floured surface. Knead dough 5 minutes or until smooth and elastic, adding additional flour to prevent sticking if necessary. Shape dough into ball; place in prepared bowl, turning dough to grease top. Cover bowl with Kwik-N-Fresh® plastic wrap; let rise in warm place 1 to 2 hours or until dough doubles in bulk.

6. Punch down dough; turn out onto lightly floured surface. Knead 10 to 12 times or until dough is smooth. Shape dough into 10-inch-long log.

7. Roll out dough into 18×8-inch rectangle with lightly floured rolling pin. Trim one ½-inch-thick strip of dough from each short (8-inch) end of rectangle; set aside strips for decorating wreath.

8. Spread almond filling evenly over dough to within 1 inch of edges. Sprinkle drained cherries and chocolate evenly over filling. Roll up dough, jelly-roll style, beginning on 18-inch side; pinch seam along length to seal.

9. Place roll, seam side down, on greased baking sheet; shape into a ring. Pinch ends together to seal. Cut dough at 1½-inch intervals to within ¾ inch of center with sharp knife. Gently lift each section and turn on its side, overlapping slices. Cover; let stand in warm place until almost doubled, about 30 minutes.

continued on page 56

Cherry, Almond & Chocolate Breakfast Wreath, continued

10. Preheat oven to 350°F. Beat remaining egg and remaining 1 tablespoon milk in small bowl with fork until well blended. Brush lightly over wreath.

11. To decorate wreath, cut 1 reserved dough strip into 15 or 18 pieces. Roll pieces into balls; place on wreath in clusters of three. Roll remaining dough strip into 12-inch long log; shape into bow. Place bow on wreath. Brush berries and bow with egg mixture.

12. Bake 30 minutes or until wreath is golden brown. (If outer edge browns more rapidly than inner edge of circle, cover outer edge with Kwik-N-Fresh® aluminum foil. Bake until inner edge is golden brown.) Cool on baking sheet 5 minutes. Remove from pan to wire rack. Cool completely. Prepare Almond Glaze; drizzle over wreath. Let stand until set. Wrap in Kwik-N-Fresh® plastic wrap. Store at room temperature up to 1 week.

Almond Glaze

Makes about ¼ cup

½ cup Sweet Harvest® powdered sugar, sifted
2 teaspoons Friendly Farms milk
¼ teaspoon almond extract

Combine all ingredients in small bowl; stir until smooth. If mixture is too thick, add additional milk 1 teaspoon at a time to thin.

ALDI

Nature's Nectar®
Cranberry Orange Coffeecake

Makes 12 servings

1½ cups biscuit baking mix
⅓ cup Sweet Harvest® granulated sugar
⅓ cup Friendly Farms sour cream
1 Goldhen® egg
2 tablespoons Nature's Nectar® 100% pure orange juice
1 tablespoon plus 1 teaspoon grated orange peel, divided
1 teaspoon Spice Club® pure vanilla
1 cup fresh or frozen whole cranberries
½ cup chopped dried fruit (such as apricots, golden raisins and figs)
⅓ cup coarsely chopped Southern Grove® walnuts
½ cup Sweet Harvest® light brown sugar
2 tablespoons Happy Farms® butter, softened
Friendly Farms aerosol whipped cream

1. Preheat oven to 350°F. Spray 12-inch tart pan with removable bottom with Ariel® no stick cooking spray.

2. Combine baking mix and granulated sugar in large bowl. Beat together sour cream, egg, orange juice, 1 tablespoon orange peel and vanilla in medium bowl. Add sour cream mixture to dry mixture; stir just until moistened. Spread into prepared pan.

3. Sprinkle cranberries, dried fruit and walnuts over batter. Stir together brown sugar, butter and remaining 1 teaspoon orange peel in small bowl; sprinkle over fruit.

4. Bake 40 to 45 minutes or until lightly browned. Serve warm with whipped cream.

Holiday Pumpkin Muffins

Makes 18 muffins

2½ cups Grandma's Best® all-purpose flour
¾ cup packed Sweet Harvest® light brown sugar
¼ cup Sweet Harvest® granulated sugar
1 tablespoon Baker's Corner® baking powder
1 teaspoon ground cinnamon
½ teaspoon ground nutmeg
½ teaspoon ground ginger
¼ teaspoon Sebree® salt
1 cup Sweet Harvest® solid-pack pumpkin
¾ cup Friendly Farms milk
½ cup Carlini® corn oil
2 Goldhen® eggs
¾ cup chopped Southern Grove® pecans
¾ cup Sweet Harvest® raisins
⅓ cup roasted, salted pumpkin seeds or chopped
    Southern Grove® pecans

1. Preheat oven to 400°F. Spray 18 standard (2½-inch) muffin pan cups with Ariel® no stick cooking spray.

2. Combine flour, sugars, baking powder, cinnamon, nutmeg, ginger and salt in large bowl. Stir pumpkin, milk, oil and eggs in medium bowl until well blended. Stir pumpkin mixture into flour mixture. Mix just until all ingredients are moistened. Stir in pecans and raisins. Spoon into prepared muffin cups, filling ⅔ full. Sprinkle pumpkin seeds over muffin batter.

3. Bake 15 to 18 minutes or until toothpick inserted into centers comes out clean. Cool in pans 10 minutes. Remove from pans; cool completely on wire racks. Store in airtight container.

Holiday Candy Cane Twists

Makes 8 servings

⅓ cup Sweet Harvest® granulated sugar
1 tablespoon ground cinnamon
1 can (11 ounces) refrigerated breadstick dough
3 tablespoons Happy Farms® butter, melted
   Red decorating icing (optional)

1. Preheat oven to 350°F. Spray baking sheet with Ariel® no stick cooking spray. Combine sugar and cinnamon in small bowl; mix well.

2. Separate dough; roll and stretch each piece of dough into 16-inch rope. Fold rope in half; twist ends together and form into candy cane shape on prepared baking sheet. Brush candy canes with butter; sprinkle with cinnamon-sugar.

3. Bake 12 to 15 minutes or until golden brown. Decorate with red icing, if desired. Serve warm.

Snowy Stationery

WHAT YOU'LL NEED
- White ink pad
- Heavy paper: red, blue, yellow
- Markers: black, orange, green, red, brown
- White ink pen

1. Coat your thumb with ink by placing it on ink pad. To make snowman patterns, stamp thumb on paper in a pleasing arrangement. If desired, stack 2 or 3 thumbprints to create snowmen bodies.

2. Use orange marker to draw carrot noses. Add eyes and mouths with black marker.

3. Add some detail by drawing holly with green marker; use red marker to add berries. If you are making snowmen bodies, use brown marker to add arms.

Use black marker to add hats. Or, draw halos with white pen to make snow angels.

4. Use white pen to write sayings on paper, such as "Let It Snow!" or "There's No People Like Snow People!"

Deutsche Küche Holiday Stollen

Makes 2 braided loaves

1½ cups (3 sticks) Happy Farms® butter, softened
4 Goldhen® egg yolks
½ cup Sweet Harvest® granulated sugar
1 teaspoon Sebree® salt
Grated peel of 1 lemon
Grated peel of 1 orange
1 teaspoon Spice Club® pure vanilla
2½ cups Friendly Farms milk, heated to 120° to 130°F
8 to 8½ cups Grandma's Best® all-purpose flour
2 packages active dry yeast
½ cup Sweet Harvest® raisins
½ cup candied lemon peel
½ cup candied orange peel
½ cup chopped red candied cherries
½ cup chopped green candied cherries
½ cup chopped Southern Grove® almonds
1 Goldhen® egg, beaten
Sweet Harvest® powdered sugar

1. Combine butter, egg yolks, granulated sugar, salt, lemon peel, orange peel and vanilla in large bowl; beat with electric mixer at medium speed until light and fluffy. Slowly add hot milk; beat until well blended. Add 2 cups flour and yeast; mix well. When mixture is smooth, add enough remaining flour, ½ cup at a time, until dough begins to pull away from side of bowl. Turn out dough onto lightly floured work surface. Knead 10 minutes or until smooth and elastic. Mix raisins, candied lemon and orange peels, cherries and almonds in medium bowl; knead fruit mixture into dough. Shape dough into ball. Place in large greased bowl; turn dough over once to grease surface. Cover with Kwik-N-Fresh® plastic wrap; let rise in warm place about 1 hour or until doubled in bulk.

2. Spray 2 large baking sheets with Ariel® no stick cooking spray. Turn dough out onto floured work surface. Divide dough in half. Cut one half into thirds. Roll each third into 12-inch rope. Place on prepared baking sheet. Braid ropes together. Repeat procedure with remaining dough. Brush braids with beaten egg. Let stand at room temperature about 1 hour or until doubled in bulk.

3. Preheat oven to 350°F. Bake braids about 45 minutes or until golden brown and sound hollow when tapped. Cool on wire racks. Sprinkle with powdered sugar.

CHAPTER 4

Homemade Holiday Gifts

Clancy's Yuletide Twisters

Makes 10 servings

6 ounces almond bark, chopped (about 1 cup)
8 ounces Clancy's twist pretzels (about 80)
  Decorations: assorted colored sugars or sprinkles

1. Line baking sheet with Kwik-N-Fresh® aluminum foil; set aside.

2. Melt almond bark in small saucepan over low heat, stirring constantly. Do not remove saucepan from heat.

3. Holding pretzel with fork, dip 1 side of pretzel into melted almond bark to coat. Place, coated side up, on prepared baking sheet; immediately sprinkle with desired decorations. Repeat with remaining pretzels. Refrigerate until firm, 15 to 20 minutes.

Chocolate Twisters: Substitute 1 cup Baker's Corner® real semisweet chocolate chips for almond bark.

Caramel Dippity Do's: Heat 1 cup caramel sauce and ⅓ cup finely chopped Southern Grove® pecans in small saucepan until warm. Pour into small serving bowl. Serve with Clancy's pretzels for dipping. Makes 8 servings.

Chocolate Dippity Do's: Heat 1 cup hot fudge sauce and ⅓ cup finely chopped Southern Grove® pecans or walnuts in small saucepan until warm. Pour into small serving bowl. Serve with Clancy's pretzels for dipping. Makes 8 servings.

Brunchtime Sour Cream Cupcakes

Makes 1¹/₂ dozen cupcakes

1 cup (2 sticks) Happy Farms® butter, softened
2 cups plus 4 teaspoons Sweet Harvest® sugar, divided
2 Goldhen® eggs
1 cup Friendly Farms sour cream
1 teaspoon almond extract
2 cups Grandma's Best® all-purpose flour
1 teaspoon Sebree® salt
½ teaspoon Baker's Corner® baking soda
1 cup chopped Southern Grove® walnuts
1½ teaspoons ground cinnamon
⅛ teaspoon ground nutmeg

1. Preheat oven to 350°F. Spray 18 standard (2¹/₂-inch) muffin pan cups with Ariel® no stick cooking spray or line with paper baking cups.

2. Beat butter and 2 cups sugar in large bowl with electric mixer at medium speed until light and fluffy. Add eggs, 1 at a time, beating well after each addition. Blend in sour cream and almond extract. Combine flour, salt and baking soda in medium bowl. Add to butter mixture; mix well.

3. Stir together remaining 4 teaspoons sugar, walnuts, cinnamon and nutmeg in small bowl.

4. Fill prepared muffin cups ¹/₃ full with batter; sprinkle about ²/₃ walnut mixture evenly over batter. Cover with remaining batter. Sprinkle with remaining walnut mixture.

5. Bake 25 to 30 minutes or until toothpick inserted into centers comes out clean. Remove cupcakes from pans; cool on wire rack.

Creamy Chocolate Marble Cheesecake

Makes 1 (9-inch) cheesecake

Cinnamon Graham Crust (recipe follows)
3 packages (8 ounces each) Happy Farms® cream cheese, softened
¾ cup Sweet Harvest® granulated sugar
3 Goldhen® eggs
1 cup Friendly Farms sour cream
1 teaspoon Spice Club® pure vanilla
¼ cup Baker's® Corner real semisweet
    chocolate chips, melted

1. Prepare Cinnamon Graham Crust.

2. Increase oven temperature to 450°F. Beat cream cheese in large bowl with electric mixer at medium speed until fluffy. Add sugar; beat until light and fluffy. Beat in eggs, 1 at a time, at low speed until well blended. Stir in sour cream and vanilla.

3. Place 1 cup batter in small bowl. Add melted chocolate; stir until well blended. Spoon plain and chocolate batters alternately over crust. To marble, cut through batters several times with knife.

4. Bake 10 minutes. *Reduce oven temperature to 250°F.* Bake 30 minutes or until center is just set. Remove pan to wire rack. Carefully loosen edge of cake with narrow knife. Cool completely on wire rack. Refrigerate several hours or overnight.

Variation (as shown): For plain cheesecake, omit melted chocolate.

Cinnamon Graham Crust

12 to 15 Sun Grams® graham crackers
3 tablespoons Sweet Harvest® granulated sugar
½ teaspoon ground cinnamon
3 tablespoons Happy Farms® butter, melted

Preheat oven to 350°F. Crush crackers to make 1 cup crumbs. Combine crumbs, sugar and cinnamon in small bowl. Stir in melted butter until blended. Press onto bottom of 9-inch springform pan. Bake 10 minutes. Cool on wire rack while preparing filling.

Cranberry Pecan Muffin Mix

Makes 1 (1-quart) gift jar

1¾ cups Grandma's Best® all-purpose flour
1 cup Fit & Active dried cranberries
¾ cup chopped Southern Grove® pecans
½ cup packed Sweet Harvest® light brown sugar
2½ teaspoons Baker's Corner® baking powder
½ teaspoon Sebree® salt

1. Layer ingredients attractively in any order in 1-quart food storage jar with tight-filling lid. Lightly pack down ingredients before adding another layer.

2. Seal jar. Cover lid with fabric; attach gift tag with preparation instructions. Decorate with raffia or ribbon.

Cranberry Pecan Muffins

Makes 12 muffins

1 jar Cranberry Pecan Muffin Mix
¾ cup Friendly Farms milk
½ cup (1 stick) Happy Farms® butter, melted
1 Goldhen® egg, beaten

1. Preheat oven to 400°F. Spray 12 standard (2½-inch) muffin pan cups with Ariel® no stick cooking spray.

2. Pour contents of jar into large bowl. Combine milk, melted butter and egg in small bowl; blend well. Add to jar mixture; stir just until moistened. Spoon evenly into prepared muffin cups.

3. Bake 16 to 18 minutes or until toothpick inserted into centers comes out clean. Cool in pan on wire rack 5 minutes. Remove from pan; cool completely on wire rack.

Choceur® Decadent Truffle Tree

Makes 1 tree (6 dozen truffles)

INGREDIENTS

1⅓ cups whipping cream
¼ cup packed Sweet Harvest® light brown sugar
¼ teaspoon Sebree® salt
¼ cup light rum (optional)
2 teaspoons Spice Club® pure vanilla
16 ounces (2¾ cups) Baker's Corner® semisweet chocolate chips
1½ bars (about 16 ounces) Choceur® Austrian milk chocolate, chopped
Finely chopped nuts and assorted sprinkles

SUPPLIES

1 (9-inch tall) foam cone
About 70 wooden toothpicks

1. Heat cream, brown sugar, salt, rum, if desired, and vanilla in medium saucepan over medium heat until sugar is dissolved and mixture is hot. Remove from heat; add chocolates, stirring until melted (return pan to low heat if necessary). Pour into shallow dish. Cover with Kwik-N-Fresh® aluminum foil; refrigerate until just firm, about 1 hour.

2. Shape half chocolate mixture into 1¼-inch balls. Shape remaining mixture into ¾-inch balls. Roll balls in nuts and sprinkles. Refrigerate truffles until firm, about 1 hour.

3. Cover cone with foil. Starting at bottom of cone, attach larger truffles with toothpicks. Use smaller truffles toward the top of the cone. Refrigerate until ready to serve.

Cook's Tip: If kitchen is very warm, keep portion of truffle mixture chilled as you shape and roll balls.

ALDI

Praline Pecans & Cranberries

Makes about 5 cups

3½ cups Southern Grove® pecan halves
¼ cup packed Sweet Harvest® light brown sugar
¼ cup Baker's Corner® light corn syrup
2 tablespoons Happy Farms® butter
1 teaspoon Spice Club® pure vanilla
¼ teaspoon Baker's Corner® baking soda
1½ cups Fit & Active dried cranberries
½ cup Baker's Corner® white chocolate chips

1. Preheat oven to 250°F. Cover large baking sheet with Kwik-N-Fresh® aluminum foil; lightly spray with Ariel® no stick cooking spray. Set aside.

2. Spray 13×9-inch baking pan with Ariel® no stick cooking spray. Spread pecans in single layer in prepared pan.

3. Combine brown sugar, corn syrup and butter in medium microwavable bowl. Microwave at HIGH 1 minute; stir. Microwave 30 seconds to 1 minute or until boiling rapidly. Carefully stir in vanilla and baking soda until well blended. Drizzle evenly over pecans; stir until evenly coated.

4. Bake 1 hour, stirring every 20 minutes with wooden spoon. Immediately transfer mixture to prepared baking sheet, spreading pecans evenly over foil with lightly greased spatula. Cool completely.

5. Break pecans apart with wooden spoon. Combine pecans, cranberries and white chocolate chips in large bowl. Store in airtight container at room temperature up to 2 weeks.

Cook's Tip: Boiling sugar syrup like the one in step 3 can cause serious burns. Add the vanilla and baking soda carefully because the syrup may boil up.

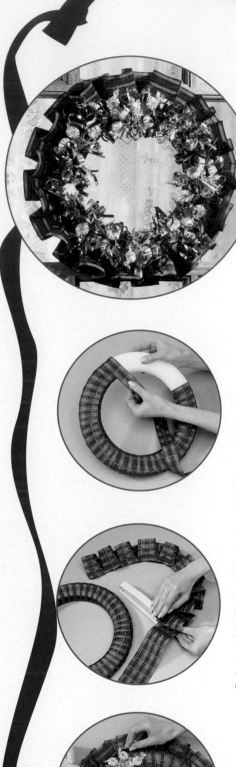

Holiday Candy Wreath

WHAT YOU'LL NEED
- **1-inch straight pins**
- **Craft glue**
- **Plastic foam wreath, 12 inches around**
- **9 yards Christmas ribbon, 2½ inches wide**
- **Scissors**
- **Stapler and staples**
- **Mystik® Starlite mints**
- **8 yards each metallic red, green, silver, gold curling ribbon, ¼ inch wide**
- **Tape measure**
- **Cloth-covered wire**

1. Dip all pins into glue before inserting into wreath. Secure 1 end of Christmas ribbon to back of foam wreath with a few straight pins. Tightly wrap wreath with ribbon to completely cover. Trim excess ribbon.

2. Use remainder of Christmas ribbon and stapler to form box pleats for around outside back of wreath. Staple pleats to hold. Pin pleats in place around wreath back.

3. Secure candy to wreath with straight pins dipped in glue. (If you want people to eat the candy, don't dip pins into glue.) Equally space candy along wreath.

4. Cut six 1-yard lengths each of red, green, silver, and gold curling ribbons. Form each length into a 6-loop bow with loops measuring 1½ inches, securing with wire. Secure each bow to wreath with pins, filling in space around candy.

5. Cut remaining curling ribbon into 6-inch lengths; curl and tie onto ends of candies randomly throughout design.

Beaded Ornament Covers

WHAT YOU'LL NEED (PER COVER)

- **Nimo D beading thread**
- **Beading needle**
- **72 bugle beads**
- **Scissors**
- **210 seed beads**
- **Round glass ornament**

1. Cut 7 feet of thread from spool. Thread it on beading needle. First round: String 18 seed beads on thread. Form a circle, and thread through circle again. Secure with a knot.

2. Second round: Place beads on needle in this order: 1 seed bead, 1 bugle bead, 1 seed bead, 1 bugle bead, 1 seed bead. Skip 2 seed beads in top circle, and insert needle into third seed bead. Repeat this step 5 more times. After you have gone through the bead on the circle for the last loop, insert needle through first half of first loop (seed bead, bugle bead, seed bead).

3. Third round: Place beads on needle in this order: 1 seed bead, 1 bugle bead, 1 seed bead, 1 bugle bead, 1 seed bead. Insert needle through center seed bead of next loop of previous round. Repeat 5 times. After you have completed the round, insert needle through first half of first loop made in this round (seed bead, bugle bead, seed bead).

4. Fourth round: Place beads on needle in this order: 1 seed bead, 1 bugle bead, 3 seed beads, 1 bugle bead, 1 seed bead. Insert needle through center seed bead of first loop of previous round. Repeat 5 times. After you have completed the round, insert needle through first half of first loop made in this round (seed bead, bugle bead, 2 seed beads).

5. Fifth round: Place beads on needle in this order: 2 seed beads, 1 bugle bead, 3 seed beads, 1 bugle bead, 2 seed beads. Insert needle through center seed bead of first loop of previous round. Repeat 5 times. After you have completed the round, insert needle through first half of first loop made in this round (2 seed beads, bugle bead, 2 seed beads).

6. Sixth round: Place beads on needle in this order: 2 seed beads, 1 bugle bead, 4 seed beads, 1 bugle bead, 1 seed bead, 1 bugle bead, 3 seed beads. Place thread around last bead and back through 2 seed beads, 1 bugle, 1 seed bead, 1 bugle bead, 2 seed beads. Place beads on needle: 2 seed beads, 1 bugle bead, 2 seed beads; and thread through center seed bead on next loop from previous round. Repeat 5 times. Secure thread with a knot after last section is attached. Work threads back into beads and knot a few more times. Cut thread. Place beading over ornament and hang to display.

CHAPTER 5

Yuletide Cakes & Pies

Choceur® White Chocolate Cranberry Tart

Makes 8 servings

1 Buehler's® refrigerated pie crust
1 cup Sweet Harvest® granulated sugar
2 Goldhen® eggs
¼ cup (½ stick) Happy Farms® butter, melted
2 teaspoons Spice Club® pure vanilla
½ cup Grandma's Best® all-purpose flour
1 bar (6 ounces) Choceur® white chocolate, chopped
½ cup chopped Southern Grove® macadamia nuts, lightly toasted*
½ cup Fit & Active dried cranberries, coarsely chopped

Toast chopped macadamia nuts in hot skillet over medium heat about 3 minutes or until fragrant.

1. Preheat oven to 350°F. Place pie crust in 9-inch tart pan with removable bottom or pie pan.

2. Combine sugar, eggs, butter and vanilla in large bowl; mix well. Stir in flour until well blended. Add white chocolate, nuts and cranberries. Pour filling into unbaked crust. Bake 50 to 55 minutes or until top of tart is crusty and deep golden brown and knife inserted into center comes out clean. Cool completely on wire rack.

Serve it with Style: Top each serving with a dollop of whipped cream flavored with ground cinnamon, a favorite liqueur and grated orange peel.

Decadent Turtle Cheesecake

Makes 1 (9-inch) cheesecake

2 cups crushed Mercer® chocolate sandwich creme cookies
    or Mercer® vanilla wafers
3 tablespoons Happy Farms® butter, melted
3 packages (8 ounces each) Happy Farms® cream cheese, softened
1 cup Sweet Harvest® granulated sugar
1 tablespoon plus 1½ teaspoons Grandma's Best® all-purpose flour
1½ teaspoons Spice Club® pure vanilla
¼ teaspoon Sebree® salt
3 Goldhen® eggs
3 tablespoons whipping cream
    Caramel and Chocolate Toppings (recipes follow)
¾ cup chopped toasted Southern Grove® pecans

1. Preheat oven to 450°F. For crust, combine cookie crumbs and butter; press onto bottom of 9-inch springform pan.

2. For filling, beat cream cheese in large bowl with electric mixer at medium speed until creamy. Beat in sugar, flour, vanilla and salt; mix well. Add eggs, 1 at a time, beating well after each addition. Blend in cream. Pour over crust.

3. Bake 10 minutes. *Reduce oven temperature to 200°F.* Continue baking 35 to 40 minutes or until set. Loosen cake from side of pan; cool completely before removing side of pan.

4. Meanwhile, prepare Caramel and Chocolate Toppings. Drizzle toppings over cheesecake. Refrigerate. Sprinkle with pecans before serving.

Caramel Topping: Combine ½ (14-ounce) bag caramels and ¼ cup whipping cream in small saucepan; stir over low heat until smooth.

Chocolate Topping: Combine 4 ounces (⅔ cup) Baker's Corner® real semisweet chocolate chips, 2 tablespoons whipping cream and 1 teaspoon Happy Farms® butter in small saucepan; stir over low heat until smooth.

Chocolate Mint Fluff Roll

Makes 8 to 10 servings

- 4 Goldhen® eggs, separated
- ¾ cup Sweet Harvest® granulated sugar, divided
- ½ cup (1 stick) Happy Farms® butter, softened
- ¼ cup crème de menthe liqueur or syrup
- 2 tablespoons water
- 1 teaspoon Spice Club® pure vanilla
- ⅔ cup cake flour
- ½ cup Baker's Corner® baking cocoa
- 1 teaspoon Baker's Corner® baking powder
- ½ teaspoon Sebree® salt
  - Sweet Harvest® powdered sugar
  - Chocolate Mint Filling (page 83)

1. Preheat oven to 375°F. Grease 15×10-inch jelly-roll pan with Carlini® vegetable shortening. Line with parchment paper and grease paper; dust with flour.

2. Beat egg whites in large bowl with electric mixer at high speed until soft peaks form. Gradually add ½ cup granulated sugar, beating until egg whites are stiff and glossy. Set aside.

3. Combine egg yolks, remaining ¼ cup granulated sugar, butter, crème de menthe, water and vanilla in small bowl. Beat about 4 minutes at medium speed or until mixture thickens. Fold yolk mixture into egg white mixture.

4. Sift flour, cocoa, baking powder and salt into medium bowl; fold flour mixture into egg mixture until blended.

5. Pour batter into prepared pan. Bake 12 to 15 minutes or until edges begin to pull away from sides of pan and center springs back when lightly touched. Dust clean linen towel with powdered sugar. Invert cake onto towel. Peel off parchment paper; starting from long side, gently roll up cake. Cool cake completely. Prepare Chocolate Mint Filling.

6. Unroll cake; spread with filling. Roll up cake and place on serving plate. Sprinkle with additional powdered sugar. Chill before serving.

Chocolate Mint Filling

1½ cups whipping cream
 ½ cup Sweet Harvest® granulated sugar
 ¼ cup Baker's Corner® baking cocoa
 ¼ cup crème de menthe liqueur or syrup
 ½ teaspoon Spice Club® pure vanilla
    Pinch Sebree® salt
1½ cups chopped chocolate mints

Combine cream, sugar, cocoa, crème de menthe, vanilla and salt in medium bowl; beat with electric mixer at high speed until stiff peaks form. Gently fold in mints.

Southern Grove® Turtle Pecan Pie

Makes 8 servings

1 cup Baker's Corner® light corn syrup
3 Goldhen® eggs, slightly beaten
⅔ cup Sweet Harvest® granulated sugar
⅓ cup Happy Farms® butter, melted
1 teaspoon Spice Club® pure vanilla
½ teaspoon Sebree® salt
1 cup toasted Southern Grove® pecans*
½ cup (3 ounces) Baker's Corner®
    real semisweet chocolate chips, melted
1 (9-inch) frozen deep dish pie crust
½ cup caramel topping
    Friendly Farms aerosol whipped cream
    Grated Choceur® Austrian milk chocolate

*To toast nuts, place on baking sheet. Bake in preheated 350°F oven 5 to 7 minutes or until lightly browned.

1. Preheat oven to 350°F.

2. Combine corn syrup, eggs, sugar, butter, vanilla and salt in large bowl; mix well. Remove ½ cup egg mixture; set aside. Stir pecans and chocolate chips into remaining egg mixture; pour into frozen pie crust.

3. Mix caramel topping and reserved egg mixture; carefully pour over pecan filling. Place pie on baking sheet. Bake 50 to 55 minutes or until filling is set about 3 inches from edge. Cool completely on wire rack.

4. Top each serving with whipped cream and grated chocolate.

Save at ALDI®

*Keep quality **ALDI**® ingredients on hand to dress up traditional desserts like pecan pie. Friendly Farms aerosol whipped cream is a must for a quick garnish. And, easily make grated or shaved chocolate by pulling a vegetable peeler across the side of a Choceur® chocolate bar. With these two simple ingredients, your desserts will be impressive and delicious.*

Celebration Pumpkin Cake

Makes 16 servings

2 packages (18.5 ounces) spice, gingerbread or carrot cake mix plus
  ingredients to prepare mixes
1 can (about 16 ounces) Sweet Harvest® solid-pack pumpkin
¼ cup (½ stick) Happy Farms® butter, softened
2 containers (16 ounces each) Baker's Corner® cream cheese frosting
⅓ cup caramel topping (page 80)
  Southern Grove® pecan halves

1. Preheat oven to 350°F. Grease 4 (9-inch) round cake pans with Carlini®
vegetable shortening; lightly flour.

2. Prepare cake mixes according to package instructions. Add pumpkin and
butter to batter; beat with electric mixer at medium speed 2 minutes. Divide
batter evenly among prepared pans. Bake 20 to 25 minutes or until toothpick
inserted into centers comes out clean. Cool 5 minutes on wire racks. Remove
from pans; cool completely.

3. Place one cake layer on serving plate; cover with frosting. Repeat layers,
ending with frosting. Frost side of cake. Spread warm caramel topping over
top of cake, letting some caramel drip down side. Garnish with pecan halves.

ALDI

Cranberry Apple Nut Pie

Makes 1 (9-inch) pie

Rich Pie Pastry (page 89)
1 cup Sweet Harvest® granulated sugar
3 tablespoons Grandma's Best® all-purpose flour
¼ teaspoon Sebree® salt
4 cups sliced peeled tart apples (4 large apples)
2 cups fresh or frozen cranberries
½ cup golden raisins
½ cup coarsely chopped Southern Grove® pecans
1 tablespoon grated lemon peel
2 tablespoons Happy Farms® butter
1 Goldhen® egg, beaten

1. Preheat oven to 425°F. Divide pie pastry in half. Roll 1 half on lightly floured surface into 13-inch circle. Fit into 9-inch pie plate; trim edges. Reroll scraps and cut into decorative shapes, such as holly leaves and berries, for garnish; set aside.

2. Combine sugar, flour and salt in large bowl. Stir in apples, cranberries, raisins, pecans and lemon peel; toss well. Spoon fruit mixture into unbaked pie crust. Dot with butter. Roll remaining half of pie pastry on lightly floured surface into 11-inch circle. Place over filling. Trim and seal edges; flute. Cut 3 slits in center of top crust. Moisten pastry cutouts and use to decorate top crust as desired. Lightly brush top crust with egg.

3. Bake 35 to 40 minutes or until apples are tender when pierced with fork and pastry is golden brown. Cool in pan on wire rack. Serve warm or cool completely.